KU-453-060

Volcanoes

Christy Steele

Nature on the Rampage

www.raintreepublishers.co.uk

Visit our website to find out more information about **Raintree** books.

To order:
- ☎ Phone 44 (0) 1865 888112
- 🖹 Send a fax to 44 (0) 1865 314091
- 💻 Visit the Raintree Bookshop at www.raintreepublishers.co.uk to browse our catalogue and order online.

First published in Great Britain by Raintree Publishers, Halley Court, Jordan Hill, Oxford, OX2 8EJ, part of Harcourt Education.
Raintree is a registered trademark of Harcourt Education Ltd.

The author wishes to thank the staff at the Cascades Volcano Observatory for their help with this book.

Raintree editorial: Isabel Thomas and Kate Buckingham
Cover design: Jo Sapwell
(www.tipani.co.uk)
Production: Jonathan Smith
Originated by Dot Gradations
Printed and bound in China by South China Printing Company

ISBN 1 844 21222 X
07 06 05 04 03
10 9 8 7 6 5 4 3 2 1

British Library Cataloguing in Publication Data
Steele, Christy
Volcanoes. - (Nature on the Rampage)
1.Volcanoes - Juvenile literature
2. Volcanism - Social aspects - Juvenile literature 3.Weather - Effect of volcanic eruptions on - Juvenile literature
I.Title
551.2'1
A full catalogue for this book is available from the British Library

Acknowledgements
The publishers would like to thank the following for permission to reproduce photographs: Dembinsky Photo Associates/S. Jonasson, p. **27**; Digital Stock, pp. **1, 4, 6, 10, 13, 16, 26, 29**; Photo Network, pp. **19, 20–21**; Visuals Unlimited/Jim Hughes, p. **15**; Peter Ziminski, p. **23**.

Cover photograph by Getty Images

Contents

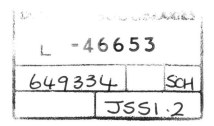

What are volcanoes?

A volcano is an opening in the Earth's surface that connects to an underground **magma** source. Magma is molten rock inside the Earth. When magma breaks through the Earth's **crust**, it forms volcanoes.

The **volcanic form** is the part of the volcano that can be seen. Volcanoes have different forms. Some volcanoes look like mountains. Others look like small hills. Some look like holes in the ground.

Volcanoes erupt. An **eruption** happens when ash, rocks, hot gas or **lava** burst through a volcano's opening. Lava is magma rock on the surface.

Lava can pile up and harden after an eruption. This builds a mountain around the volcano's opening.

crust

Layers of the Earth

The Earth is made up of three layers. The **core** is the centre of the Earth. It is made of very hot, heavy rock and metal. The mantle is the middle layer of the Earth. It is also made of rock. Parts of the mantle melt and make magma. The crust is the thin, outer layer of the Earth. It is cooler and made of light rocks. If the Earth were egg-sized, the crust would be as thick as the shell.

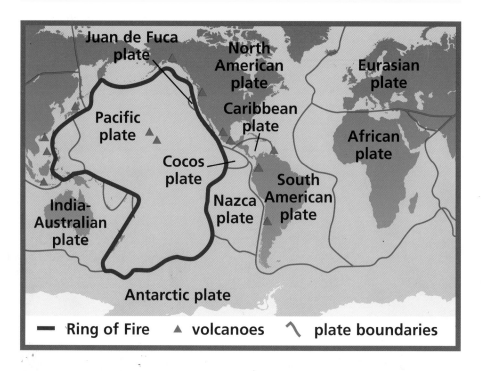

Juan de Fuca plate
North American plate
Eurasian plate
Pacific plate
Caribbean plate
African plate
Cocos plate
South American plate
India-Australian plate
Nazca plate
Antarctic plate

— Ring of Fire   ▲ volcanoes   ⌐ plate boundaries

Where do volcanoes form?

Volcanoes are found on land and under water. They start at cracks or weak places on the crust. Some parts of the crust are thinner than others. The thin parts of the crust can be weak.

Other weak places occur because of the Earth's plates. A plate is a giant piece of the Earth's crust. Scientists believe that many plates fit together like puzzle pieces to make up the Earth's crust.

Plates move. They slide over magma in the **mantle**. The plates' movements may make cracks in the crust. Most cracks happen where two moving plates meet each other.

The Pacific Plate moves past many other plates. This plate's movements have caused most of the world's volcanoes to form around its edges. People call the edges of the Pacific Plate the Ring of Fire because of its many volcanoes.

 This diagram shows the main plates that make up the Earth's crust. Volcanoes often start at plate edges.

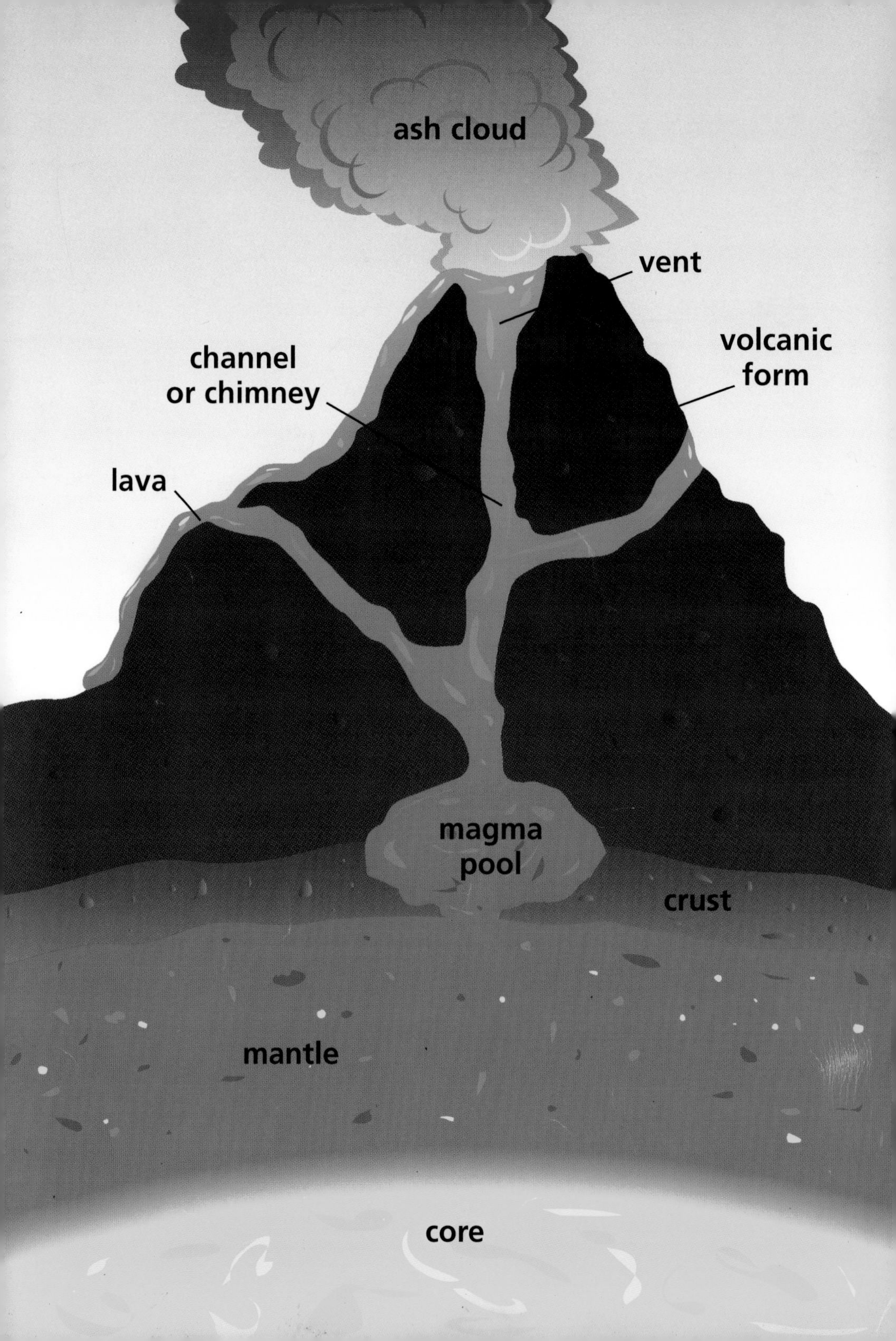

ash cloud

vent

volcanic
form

channel
or chimney

lava

magma
pool

crust

mantle

core

Parts of a volcano

Every volcano must have a source of magma. Magma is lighter than solid rock. It rises from the mantle and flows towards the Earth's surface. Magma sometimes collects under the surface in a pool. A volcano may have several of these **magma pools**.

Another part of a volcano is its **channel**, or chimney. A channel is a pipe-like tunnel that goes from the mantle to the crust's surface. Magma flows up from the mantle through the channel. A volcano may have many channels.

A **vent** is the opening at the top of a volcano's channel. The vent opens to the Earth's surface.

Eruptions create the volcanic form. During eruptions lava, gas, rock and ash clouds can escape from the vent. Once magma reaches the vent, it is called lava. Over time, the lava hardens. The rocks, ash and hard lava make a volcanic form around the vent.

The volcano's form changes after each eruption. New lava and ash may pile on top of the old material. This will make the form taller and thicker.

◀ **This diagram shows the parts of a volcano.**

Volcanic eruptions

Several things can cause volcanic eruptions. Plate movements may start eruptions. Earthquakes can start eruptions. Earthquakes can open new cracks in the crust. Lava can then erupt through the new cracks.

Volcanoes can have different kinds of eruptions. Hot steam and gases such as carbon dioxide, sulphur dioxide and hydrogen escape during small eruptions. Other eruptions release large clouds of ash as well as these gases. During some eruptions, lava spits from cracks and forms lava streams. Lava, ash, gas and rocks explode into the air during large eruptions.

This volcano in Hawaii is having a small eruption of hot steam and gases.

Volcanic flows

Huge streams of lava make up lava flows. Lava can be thick or thin. Thick lava moves slowly and does not travel far. People usually have time to move away from the path of a thick lava flow. Thin lava covers large areas quickly. People often do not have time to escape from a thin lava flow.

Lava flows can burn or bury everything in their paths. Since 1983, lava flows in Hawaii have buried more than 200 houses.

A **pyroclastic flow** is a mixture of hot gas, ash and stones. Pyroclastic flows are fast and deadly. They can get as hot as 815°C (1500°F). They rush down volcanoes at speeds of up to 100 kilometres (60 miles) an hour. These flows destroy anything in their path.

Heavy rain or melting snow and ice can start mudflows. These flows are made of mud, rock and water. Mudflows can travel at over 100 kilometres (60 miles) an hour. They can spread up to 80 kilometres (50 miles).

This lava flow in Hawaii has buried everything in its path. The top of the flow has cooled and hardened.

Damage from volcanoes

Small eruptions do little harm. The escaped steam and gas simply mix with the air. But large eruptions can cause serious harm and create damaging flows.

Great amounts of ash escape into the air during large eruptions. Wind can blow clouds of ash far from erupting volcanoes. Since 1983, over 80 aeroplanes have been damaged by flying into ash clouds. Huge ash clouds can change the weather by blocking some of the sun's rays. Some large ash clouds can make the weather colder for a year or more. Colder weather may damage crops.

Falling ash can be heavy. It can cover roofs and make them fall down. This can crush people inside buildings. Falling ash can fill lakes. The water then mixes with the ash and turns to mud. All the fish and plants in the lake die.

During large eruptions, rocks of all sizes are ejected into the air from the volcano. Large falling rocks can kill people and animals.

Lava flows cause lots of damage. Lava flows can start fires. Mudflows rip up trees and houses and bury everything in their paths. Pyroclastic flows can destroy entire forests.

▲ A pyroclastic flow destroyed this forest in Washington State, USA.

Volcanic eruptions underwater can cause tsunamis. Tsunamis are huge waves that travel a long way across oceans. They cause great floods when they wash over land (see *Tsunamis* in this series).

Volcanoes in history

The name volcano comes from the Roman god of fire. His name was Vulcan. Romans believed he lived underneath a mountain on a small island in the Mediterranean Sea. The mountain erupted fire. Romans called the island Vulcano. Today, all mountains that erupt are called volcanoes after the mythological god Vulcan.

People on the Hawaiian Islands believed the goddess Pele made volcanoes. Pele could change herself into lava. Pele stamped her feet or dug with her magic stick when she was angry. These actions made volcanoes erupt.

Scientists call smooth lava pahoehoe. **This Hawaiian lava flow shows what hardening pahoehoe looks like.**

Vesuvius eruption in AD 79

Mount Vesuvius in Italy erupted on 24 to 25 August in the year AD 79. A huge cloud of ash rose into the sky. Vesuvius erupted ash clouds and started many pyroclastic flows.

Ash and stones fell on the nearby town of Pompeii. The stones made roofs and buildings fall down on people. Many people left the town. On 25 August, Vesuvius erupted a cloud of ash and poisonous gas. It rushed through Pompeii. Everyone who was left in the town died.

Herculaneum was another small town near Mount Vesuvius. On 25 August AD 79, a thick mudflow and a pyroclastic flow of hot ash, rock and poisonous gas exploded from Vesuvius. The flows quickly buried Herculaneum under 20 metres of rock and mud. Everyone left in Herculaneum died.

Tambora eruption in 1815

On 10 April 1815, the Indonesian volcano Tambora erupted. The volcano spat rock and ash into the sky. Stones and ash fell on nearby cities. A pyroclastic flow ripped apart houses and uprooted trees.

About 92,000 people died. Some died in the

Ash hardened around the bodies of people who died in Pompeii. The bodies decayed and left hollows in the ash. Scientists have poured plaster into the hollows to make moulds.

eruption. Others died afterwards from lack of food. The eruption killed crops. Tambora was the deadliest eruption in recorded history.

Tambora's ash cloud made the weather around the world about six degrees colder than average during the following year. In North America, it was called 'the year without a summer'. It snowed in the eastern USA in June 1815. The cold weather killed many crops around the world.

Mount Pelée is still an active volcano. It may erupt again someday.

Mount Pelée eruption in 1902

Mount Pelée is a volcano on the Caribbean island of Martinique. In February 1902, smoke and ash poured out of Pelée. Animals tried to escape the volcano's ash. Ants, centipedes and snakes invaded the nearby town of St Pierre. About 50 people and 200 animals died from insect and snake bites.

On 8 May 1902, Mount Pelée erupted a huge cloud of hot ash, steam and poisonous gas. This pyroclastic flow moved quickly into St Pierre. It blasted buildings and started fires. The hot gas and steam burnt people's skin. People breathed in the poisonous gas and died.

About 30,000 people died. Only two people in St Pierre lived through the eruption. One was a shoemaker living on the edge of the town away from the poisonous gases. The other man was a prisoner in an underground cell.

Mount Saint Helens eruption in 1980

The serious study of volcanoes began after the Pelée eruption. This science is called volcanology. Volcanologists are scientists who study volcanoes.

Mount Saint Helens is a volcano in the state of Washington, in the USA. For 123 years, the volcano was resting. On 27 March, 1980, the volcano had a small eruption. It blew out steam and ash. Other small eruptions followed.

Volcanologists studied Mount Saint Helens. They looked at its ash and gas. Scientists saw that the volcano was growing by about 2 metres every day. Volcanologists believed Saint Helens might have a large eruption. They warned people living near the volcano.

On 18 May 1980, an avalanche made Mount Saint Helens erupt. An avalanche is a large amount of snow, ice or soil that falls down a mountain. The volcano's summit slid away in the avalanche releasing pressure from the magma system. This caused a huge landslide and triggered a powerful explosion.

A pyroclastic flow destroyed many places around Mount Saint Helens.

The explosion blasted smoke, steam and ash into the sky. A pyroclastic flow carried ash, steam and rocks for about 370 kilometres (230 miles). It destroyed trees and buildings.

The eruption killed more than 50 people. This eruption was the worst volcanic disaster in the history of North America.

Volcanoes and science

About 500 active volcanoes exist around the world. An active volcano is a volcano that has erupted at least once in recorded history. More than half the world's active volcanoes are in the Pacific Ocean in the Ring of Fire.

Volcanologists study these active volcanoes. They want to learn more about how volcanoes work. They also want to learn how to predict better when volcanoes will erupt. Then they can warn people. Better warnings can help save people's lives.

Lava from a volcano in Hawaii is making steam as it flows into the ocean. Hawaii has many active volcanoes.

Volcano safety

Today, scientists can sometimes tell that a volcano is going to erupt. Officials may issue a volcano warning. This means a volcano is about to erupt. People can save their lives by evacuating during volcanic warnings. Evacuate means to leave quickly.

Sometimes volcanoes erupt without warning. People should then take shelter inside strong buildings with closed windows. This will give them some protection from ash and gases. People should use wet cloths to cover their mouths and noses. Breathing or swallowing dust or ash can be deadly.

People should stay away from the ocean if a volcano erupts. An eruption could cause a flood or a tsunami. Tsunamis might wash over the land.

Equipment used by volcanologists

Scientists have invented equipment to help them study volcanoes. They wear special suits to protect themselves. These suits will not catch fire. They wear heavy boots to protect their feet from heat.

Volcanologists put seismometers near a volcano. Seismometers help scientists to tell when earthquakes have happened. Earthquakes often come before a volcano erupts.

▲ **People have evacuated this area in Iceland because a volcano is erupting.**

Tilt-meters measure how much volcanoes grow. Volcanoes often grow before they erupt.

Volcanologists use thermometers to measure a volcano's temperature. Volcanoes get hotter before they erupt.

Good things about volcanoes

Volcanic eruptions are important to the Earth because they create new crust. Lava hardens to form volcanic rock. Volcanic rock makes up most of the Earth's crust. Large volcanoes rise up from ocean floors to form islands. For example, volcanoes created the islands of Hawaii and Iceland.

A volcano's hot water and steam give off heat. People in Iceland put pipes underground near hot lava flows. They pump water through the pipes to heat their homes.

Lava flows and volcanic ash add minerals to the soil. These minerals help plants grow. Farmers raise crops near volcanoes.

Some people are trying to control lava flows. In Italy, the government bombed lava flows to change their paths. In Iceland, villagers sprayed lava flows with cold water to cool them and slow them down. People someday may learn new ways to reduce the damage from volcanic eruptions.

This lava flow is hardening into black volcanic rock. Igneous rock is another name for volcanic rock.

Glossary

channel pipe-like opening through which magma flows up to a volcano's vent

core centre of the Earth; very hot metals make up the Earth's core.

crust outer layer of the Earth

eruption when lava, gas, rock and ash escapes through a volcano's vent

lava (LAH-vuh) molten rock that has escaped from a volcano to the Earth's surface

magma hot, molten rock inside the Earth

magma pool huge pool of magma in the Earth's mantle

mantle middle layer of the Earth; thick, heavy rocks make up the mantle

pahoehoe (puh-HO-ay-ho-ay) Polynesian word scientists use to describe the surface of smooth lava flows

pyroclastic flow (Pi-roe-CLAS-tick) volcano flow made of hot gas, ash and stones

vent opening at the top of a volcano's channel; lava and gas erupt through the vent

volcanic form the part of a volcano that can be seen

Addresses and Internet sites

British Geological Survey Headquarters
Kingsley Dunham Centre
Keyworth
Nottingham, NG12 5GG

Italy's volcanoes
boris.vulcanoetna.com

Savage Earth
www.pbs.org/wnet/savageearth

Volcanoes Online
library.thinkquest.org/17457/english.html

Volcano World
www.volcanoworld.org/

How Volcanoes Work
www.howstuffworks.com/volcano.htm

Riddle of Pompeii
www.channel4.com/history/microsites/P/pompeii/

Index